CogAT® Practice Test

CogAT® Practice Test Levels 9 and 10 (Form 7)

Written and published by: Bright Kids NYC

Copyright © 2012 by Bright Kids NYC Inc. All of the questions in this book have been created by the staff and consultants of Bright Kids NYC Inc.

The *Cognitive Abilities Test* (*CogAT*®) is a registered trademark of Houghton Mifflin Company, which was not involved in the production of, and neither endorses nor supports the content of this *CogAT*® Practice Test.

All rights reserved. No part of this book may be reproduced or transmitted in any form or by any means without written permission from the author. ISBN (978-1-935858-71-3)

Corporate Headquarters:
Bright Kids NYC Inc.
225 Broadway
Suite 1504
New York, NY 10007
www.brightkidsnyc.com
info@brightkidsnyc.com
917-539-4575

CogAT® Practice Test - Table of Contents

About Bright Kids NYC	5
Introduction	7
CogAT® Form 7 Overview	9
CogAT® Form 7 Content and Format	11
CogAT® Form 7 Subtest Descriptions	13
Scoring Guidelines	15
General Administration Guidelines	17
Getting Ready	19
Test One – Verbal Analogies	23
Test Two – Sentence Completion	31
Test Three – Verbal Classifications	39
Test Four – Number Analogies	47
Test Five – Number Puzzles	55
Test Six – Number Series	65
Test Seven – Figure Matrices	73
Test Eight – Paper Folding	85
Test Nine – Figure Classification	95
Answer Keys	105
Answer Sheets	109

About Bright Kids NYC

Bright Kids NYC was founded in New York City to provide language arts and math enrichment for young children. Our goal is to prepare students of all ages for standardized exams through assessments, tutoring workshops, and our publications. Our philosophy is that, regardless of age, test taking is a skill that can be acquired and mastered through practice.

At Bright Kids NYC, we strive to provide the best learning materials. Our publications are truly unique. All of our books have been created by qualified psychologists, learning specialists, teachers, and staff writers. Our books have also been tested by hundreds of children in our tutoring practice. Since children can make associations that many adults cannot, testing of materials by children is a critical step towards creating successful test preparation guides. Finally, our learning specialists and teaching staff have provided practical strategies and tips to help students compete successfully on standardized exams.

Feel free to contact us should you have any questions.

Corporate Headquarters:
Bright Kids NYC Inc.
225 Broadway
Suite 1504
New York, NY 10007
www.brightkidsnyc.com
info@brightkidsnyc.com
917-539-4575

Introduction

Bright Kids NYC created the *CogAT®* Practice Test to familiarize students with the content and format of the *CogAT®*. Students, no matter how bright they may be, do not always perform well if they are not accustomed to the format and structure of a standardized exam. They can misunderstand the directions or fail to carefully read a question and properly consider all of the answer choices. Thus, without adequate preparation and familiarization, a student may not perform to the best of his or her ability on a standardized exam like the *CogAT®*.

The Bright Kids *CogAT®* Practice Test is not designed to generate a score or a percentile rank since the test has not been standardized with actual *CogAT®* norms and standards. The objective of the practice test is to identify a student's strengths, weaknesses, and overall test-taking ability in order to adequately prepare him or her for the actual exam.

In order to maximize the effectiveness of the Bright Kids *CogAT®* Practice Test, it is important for the student to first familiarize him- or herself with the test and its instructions. In addition, it is recommended that he or she designates a quiet place to work in a neutral environment free of noise and clutter. Finally, a comfortable seating arrangement will help a student focus and concentrate to the best of his or her ability.

Most students will have to take numerous standardized exams throughout their school years. The best way to develop the critical thinking skills for these types of exams is to practice with similarly styled exams under test-like conditions. This method helps ensure that a student will succeed on his or her exam.

CogAT® Form 7 Overview

The *Cognitive Abilities Test* (*CogAT®*) is designed to evaluate the level and pattern of cognitive development of students in grades K through 12. It is important to note that the *CogAT®* measures developed cognitive abilities, not innate cognitive abilities. The development of these cognitive abilities begins at birth and continues through early adulthood. These abilities are vastly influenced by both in-school and out-of-school life experiences. Since these cognitive abilities are closely related to a student's academic success, the *CogAT®* test results may be used to help shape a student's curriculum at his or her school. The *CogAT®* test results are also used to identify students who may belong in Gifted and Talented programs.

The *CogAT®* is based on several theoretical models of human intelligence and assessment. In 1904, Charles Spearman proposed that human intelligence is composed of a general reasoning ability factor (called "g") and specific cognitive abilities (called "s-factors"). Raymond Cattell concluded in 1963 that g is composed of fluid and crystallized intelligence. Fluid intelligence is independent of acquired knowledge. It includes spatial and visual imagery skills, reasoning ability, memory capacity, and information processing. Fluid intelligence is the capacity to reason logically in new and unique situations. Crystallized intelligence is the use of acquired knowledge to solve various types of problems. Crystallized intelligence increases with age as a person gains more concrete knowledge and experience. In 1960, John Vernon proposed a hierarchical model of intelligence where g is at the top. On the next level, there are verbal/educational skills and practical/mechanical/spatial skills.

The *CogAT®* is primarily influenced by Vernon's and Cattell's theoretical models of cognitive abilities since it measures both general and specific reasoning abilities. On the *CogAT®*, g is operationally defined as the abstract and inductive reasoning skills that are fundamental for acquiring, organizing, and storing knowledge. These skills are tested on every domain of the exam. The Nonverbal Battery seeks to assess the practical/mechanical/spatial skills and fluid intelligence of the student. The Verbal and Quantitative Batteries on the exam appraise the verbal/educational skills and crystallized intelligence of the student. The clusters of the scores on these batteries become much more differentiated and more closely related to specific kinds of learning tasks as a student grows older. Each battery on the exam has three different reasoning tasks to ensure the dependability of the reported score for each student.

CogAT® Form 7 Content

The *Cognitive Abilities Test (CogAT®)* is designed to evaluate students' general and specific cognitive abilities. Schools may use these scores to help establish instructional objectives for each grade. Since the primary purpose of the *CogAT®* is to provide a description of the mental abilities of a student, several reasoning tests appraise a student's general cognitive skills using verbal, quantitative, and nonverbal tasks. The *CogAT®*7 has been updated from the *CogAT®*6 to reduce the oral vocabulary portion of the exam; this is meant to diminish the bias towards students who speak English as a second language.

Every level of the *CogAT®*7 contains a Verbal, Quantitative, and a Nonverbal Battery. In each battery, there are three subtests. For the Verbal Battery, the subtests are Picture/Verbal Analogies, Sentence Completion, and Picture/Verbal Classification. For the Quantitative Battery, the subtests are Number Analogies, Number Puzzles, and Number Series. For the Nonverbal Battery, the subtests are Figure Matrices, Paper Folding, and Figure Classification.

The multiple levels on the *CogAT®*7 correspond to the different grades of students who take the exam. The Primary Edition, Levels 5/6-8, of the *CogAT®*7 is designed to test students in Kindergarten through Second Grade. No reading is required on the Primary Edition; all directions are read aloud by an examiner who also paces the students through the questions. Most of the items are picture-based and not specifically tied to the English language. The structure and format of the Primary Edition test items in Form 7 have been altered from Form 6 to create more consistency with the Multilevel Edition.

The Multilevel Edition, Levels 9-17/18, of the *CogAT®*7 is designed to test students in Third through Twelfth Grade. Level 9 is the transition point where the test shifts from picture-based verbal and quantitative items to text- and numeric-based verbal and quantitative items. Level 9 is also the point where students must complete each subtest on their own in a timed situation. Students will have ten minutes to complete each subtest.

The *CogAT®*7 subtests are constructed in a modular format. Easy items are dropped and more difficult items are added as one moves across levels. The abstract reasoning skills appraised across all of the subtests include the ability to organize and remember information, make inferences and detect relationships, comprehend and analyze problem situations, form concepts, discover and remember sequences, recognize patterns, classify or categorize objects and events, infer rules and principles, and to relate previous experience to new tasks and problems.

CogAT® Form 7 Levels 9-10 Subtest Descriptions

Verbal Battery

The Levels 9-10 Verbal Battery items consist of Verbal Analogies, Sentence Completion, and Verbal Classification subtests. In the **Verbal Analogies** subtest, the student is given two words and he/she must determine the relationship between the two words. Once the student has determined the relationship, he/she must apply the same relationship to a different word in order to determine which answer choice belongs after the arrow in the question. In the **Sentence Completion** subtest, the student must choose the word that best completes the sentence. In the **Verbal Classification** subtest, a student is given three words that can be classified in a certain way. He/She must choose the answer choice that correctly belongs with this group of words.

Quantitative Battery

The Levels 9-10 Quantitative Battery items consist of Number Analogies, Number Puzzles, and Number Series subtests. In the **Number Analogies** subtest, the student must use the same process he/she used in the Verbal Analogies subtest to determine the correct relationship for each pair of numbers. Once the student has determined the correct relationship, he/she must apply the same relationship to a different number to determine which answer choice belongs after the arrow in the question. In the **Number Puzzles** subtest, the student must choose the number that can be placed in the empty box to make both sides of the equation equal. In the **Number Series** subtest, the student is given a series of numbers which increase or decrease in a certain pattern. He/She needs to choose the number that belongs after the arrow in the series. On the actual Level 9 Number Series subtest, the first few questions will each have a picture of an abacus to the left of the number series. This is meant to act as a visual aid to the student. Later in the Level 9 Number Series subtest, the questions only contain different series of numbers. There are no visual aids on the Level 10 Number Series subtest. In this practice exam, these visual aids are not present since students for both levels of the exam will have to deal with number series without visual aids at some point in their respective subtests.

Nonverbal Battery

The Nonverbal Battery consists of Figure Matrices, Paper Folding and Figure Classifications. In the **Figure Matrices** subtest, students must follow the same process they did in the Verbal and Number Analogies subtests, but instead of words or numbers, the questions in this subtest utilize figural shapes to test the students' spatial skills. In the **Paper Folding** subtest, students must visualize what happens when a piece of paper is folded, cut in some way, and then unfolded. In the **Figural Classifications** subtest, students are presented with three or four figures. Then, they must select the figure among the answer choices that belongs with the set of figures.

CogAT® Practice Test

TABLE 1: Distribution of Types of Questions [1]

SUBTEST	Level 5/6	Level 7	Level 8	Level 9	Levels 10 -17/18
Grade	K	1st	2nd	3rd	4th to 11th
Verbal Battery					
Picture/Verbal Analogies	14	16	18	22	24
Sentence Completion	14	16	18	20	20
Picture/Verbal Classifications	14	16	18	20	20
Quantitative Battery					
Number Analogies	14	16	18	18	18
Number Puzzles	10	12	14	16	16
Number Series	14	16	18	18	18
Nonverbal Battery					
Figure Matrices	14	16	18	20	22
Paper Folding	10	12	16	16	16
Figure Classification	14	16	18	20	22
Total	**118**	**136**	**156**	**170**	**176**

---

[1] This may or may not represent the question mix of the actual *CogAT®* test, as the mix among different types of questions may change from test to test.

Scoring Guidelines

CogAT® test results provide a wealth of useful information. The scores can be used as follows:

1) To create individualized instruction: Each student gets a score report that includes stanines, relative strengths and weaknesses, and extreme score differences.

2) To identify gifted students: The high ceiling on the *CogAT®* allows for reliable discrimination among the top 10 percent of scores in all age groups.

3) To predict achievement: The *CogAT®* has been normed with the Iowa Test of Basic Skills® (ITBS®) and the Iowa Tests of Educational Development®. The joint norming of the *CogAT®* with elementary and secondary school achievement tests means that the *CogAT®* can predict the likely achievement levels of students on similar standardized exams.

4) To identify at-risk students.

5) To evaluate current and new curricula.

Each child receives a composite or a total score on the *CogAT®* as well as a stanine or a percentile rank. The composite or total score indicates the overall strength of the student's cognitive resources for learning. As the level of the composite score decreases, the variety and strength of the student's cognitive resources also decrease and the need for help with learning increases. Students with an above average, or very high composite score, have an array of strongly developed cognitive resources. They usually learn quickly and typically do not need special help to achieve instructional objectives. Students with a below average, or very low composite score, have very weak cognitive resources, learn very slowly, and need considerable assistance to achieve instructional objectives.

The Bright Kids *CogAT®* Practice Test can only be scored by the total number of correct answers, or the overall raw score. Since this practice test has not been standardized with the *CogAT®*, scaled scores, stanines, or percentile ranks cannot be obtained from the raw score. The purpose of this practice test is to familiarize a student with the exam and to help evaluate his/her strengths and weaknesses on each individual subtest. Please realize that a student can miss many questions on the actual exam and still obtain a high score.

General Administration Guidelines

The test is typically administered in two or three different sittings. A short rest period is recommended if more than two subtests are administered in one sitting.

The recommended timeline is as follows:

First Sitting

Distributing Materials & Practice Questions	*Approximately 5 minutes*
Test 1: Verbal Analogies	Approximately 10 minutes
Test 2: Sentence Completion	Approximately 10 minutes
Test 3: Verbal Classification	Approximately 10 minutes

Second Sitting

Distributing Materials & Practice Questions	*Approximately 5 minutes*
Test 4: Number Analogies	Approximately 10 minutes
Test 5: Number Puzzles	Approximately 10 minutes
Test 6: Number Series	Approximately 10 minutes

Third Sitting

Distributing Materials & Practice Questions	*Approximately 5 minutes*
Test 7: Figure Matrices	Approximately 10 minutes
Test 8: Paper Folding	Approximately 10 minutes
Test 9: Figure Classification	Approximately 10 minutes

Getting Ready

Materials

1. Several No. 2 soft lead pencils, erasers, and pencil sharpeners.

2. Ideally, a "Do Not Disturb" sign for the room where the test will be administered.

3. A timer or clock.

4. The answer sheet, located in the back of this book.

Prior to Testing

1. The student should familiarize him- or herself with the instructions for each subtest.

2. A parent or teacher should make sure that there is ample lighting and ventilation in the room where the test will be administered.

3. The student should take the test in a room free from distractions.

During Testing

1. The student should make sure that he/she is on the correct subtest section on his/her answer sheet. He/She should also make sure that the bubbles being filled in on the answer sheet correspond to the correct question numbers in the test booklet.

2. The student should take care to completely fill in the bubble for each question on the answer sheet.

3. The student should only take ten minutes to complete each subtest of the exam.

4. The student should not receive any feedback while he/she is taking the exam. Once the testing is complete, a parent or teacher can go over the answers with the student.

5. A parent or teacher may want to consider providing positive reinforcements to ensure that the student completes the test to the best of his/her ability.

Bright Kids NYC
CogAT® Form 7 Practice Test

Levels 9 and 10
Grades 3 and 4

CogAT® is a registered trademark of Houghton Mifflin Company. Houghton Mifflin neither endorses nor supports the content of this *CogAT®* Practice Test. No parts of this practice test may be reproduced or transmitted in any form or by any means without written permission from Bright Kids NYC Inc. ISBN (978-1-935858-71-3).

Test 1:
Verbal Analogies

Test 1: Verbal Analogies

Directions

For each question on this subtest, you need to figure out the relationship between the first pair of words before the colon mark. Then, you must apply the same relationship to the word after the colon mark in order to determine which word belongs after the arrow.

S1   in → out : left →

A. right   B. side   C. in   D. direction   E. bottom

The first two words are **in** and **out**. How are these two words related to one another? In is the opposite of out. Now, look at the word after the colon mark. What is the opposite of left? The opposite of left is **right. Answer choice (A)** is correct.

Find the **Test 1: Verbal Analogies** section on your answer sheet. The first row of bubbles in this section is marked **S1**. Fill in the bubble labeled "A" in this row on your answer sheet.

Try to answer the second sample question on your own.

S2   hammer → nail : bat →

A. base   B. field   C. ball   D. drink   E. pretzel

The correct answer is **answer choice (C), ball**. You use a hammer to hit a nail and you use a bat to hit a ball. You should have filled in the bubble labeled "C" on the row marked **S2** on your answer sheet.

For all of the questions on this subtest, you need to determine how the first pair of words goes together. Then, you must apply the same relationship to the word after the colon mark to determine which answer choice belongs after the arrow in the question.

Mark all of your answers in the **Test 1: Verbal Analogies** section on your answer sheet. Make sure that you are on the correct question number on your answer sheet whenever you circle in your answer.

You will have ten minutes to complete this subtest. Try to answer every question. If you have trouble with a question, make an educated guess and move on to the next question. If you have time, you can go back to work on the questions you had trouble with. If you finish the Verbal Analogies subtest early, you may check your work but do not go on to the next subtest.

On the Level 9 Verbal Analogies subtest, there are only 22 questions. Students who plan on taking the Level 9 exam may choose to stop after question #22 in this subtest. Students who plan on taking the Level 10 exam must attempt to answer all 24 questions in this subtest.

CogAT® Practice Test - Verbal Analogies

1. finger → hand : toe →

   A. finger   B. foot   C. bone   D. leg   E. nail

2. shell → egg : peel →

   A. fruit   B. banana   C. knife   D. strawberry   E. bread

3. church → religion : stadium →

   A. peanuts   B. grass   C. athletes   D. sports   E. fun

4. up → down : above →

   A. below   B. round   C. beside   D. outside   E. near

5. cat → kitten : goat →

   A. kid   B. fawn   C. chick   D. animal   E. milk

6. car → garage : ship →

   A. water   B. station   C. dock   D. sail   E. engine

7. see → glasses : walk →

   A. old   B. run   C. leg   D. cane   E. person

8. feather → bird : scale →

   A. octopus   B. weight   C. measurement   D. fish   E. animal

Bright Kids NYC Inc. ©   CogAT® Practice Test – Levels 9 and 10

CogAT® Practice Test - Verbal Analogies

9. clock → time : thermometer →

A. hot   B. cold   C. instrument   D. distance   E. temperature

10. pillowcase → pillow : envelope →

A. stamp   B. letter   C. postage   D. address   E. buy

11. hair → brush : floor →

A. pull   B. sweep   C. handle   D. squeeze   E. rake

12. swim → water : ski →

A. snowboard   B. mountain   C. cold   D. race   E. snow

13. shoelace → shoe : zipper →

A. jacket   B. hat   C. sock   D. heel   E. toe

14. hat → head : sandals →

A. shoes   B. feet   C. beach   D. walk   E. socks

15. fish → bowl : bird →

A. jungle   B. talk   C. cage   D. zoo   E. fly

16. swim → pool : bowl →

A. line   B. alley   C. ball   D. kitchen   E. score

17. aunt → uncle : niece →

A. sister B. daughter C. nephew D. brother E. family

18. geese → migrate : bears →

A. sleep B. forest C. run D. hide E. hibernate

19. librarians → books : botanists →

A. plants B. stars C. birds D. garden E. rock

20. sailboat → sail : car →

A. wheel B. road C. ocean D. driver E. wind

21. joke → laugh : insult →

A. cry B. sleep C. hungry D. exercise E. taunt

22. hamper → clothes : canteen →

A. pitcher B. glass C. vase D. water E. desert

23. scramble → egg : mash →

A. potato B. mix C. crush D. bread E. store

24. minestrone → soup : iceberg →

A. salad B. cold C. pasta D. arctic E. lettuce

Test 2:
Sentence Completion

Test 2: Sentence Completion

Directions

For each question on this subtest, you need to choose the word that best completes the sentence. Read the sentence below and choose the answer choice that makes the most sense in the sentence.

S1   Dogs have four legs and one _____.

A. eye   B. hair   C. bark   D. tail   E. person

The correct answer choice is **(D) tail**. The sentence should read: **Dogs have four legs and one tail**. None of the other answer choices make sense when they are inserted into the sentence.

Find the **Test 2: Sentence Completion** section on your answer sheet. The first row of bubbles in this section is marked **S1**. Fill in the bubble labeled "D" in this row on your answer sheet.

Try to answer the second sample question on your own.

S2   Fiona _____ after her friend told her a funny joke.

A. walked   B. laughed   C. cried   D. ran   E. shouted

The correct answer is **(B) laughed**. The sentence should read: **Fiona laughed after her friend told her a funny joke**. You should have filled in the bubble labeled "B" on the row marked **S2** on your answer sheet.

For all of the questions on this subtest, you need to choose the word that best completes the sentence. Read the sentence for each question and choose the answer choice that makes the most sense in the sentence.

Mark all of your answers in the **Test 2: Sentence Completion** section on your answer sheet. Make sure that you are on the correct question number on your answer sheet whenever you circle in your answer.

You will have ten minutes to complete this subtest. Try to answer every question. If you have trouble with a question, make an educated guess and move on to the next question. If you have time, you can go back to work on the questions you had trouble with. If you finish the Sentence Completion subtest early, you may check your work but do not go on to the next subtest.

CogAT® Practice Test - Sentence Completion

1. Due to the torrential _____, all of the streets were closed.

A. construction   B. party   C. politician   D. accident   E. rain

2. We exercise in the _____ inside our school.

A. field   B. gym   C. floor   D. classroom   E. locker room

3. The kitchen had just been cleaned and the counter looked _____.

A. bland   B. messy   C. organized   D. unkempt   E. happy

4. After running the marathon, Sarah was _____ and tired.

A. angry   B. energetic   C. bored   D. interested   E. sore

5. Looking back, I have so many great _____ of summer camp.

A. friends   B. memories   C. emotions   D. adventures   E. crafts

6. People _____ forget to put the cap back on the toothpaste.

A. never   B. often   C. should   D. do not   E. only

7. Mary wanted to put the cake in the _____, but the cookies were still baking.

A. oven   B. microwave   C. closet   D. dining room   E. cabinet

8. The doctor tried to calm his scared _____ before the operation.

A. patient   B. nurse   C. sister   D. glasses   E. friend

Bright Kids NYC Inc. ©   CogAT® Practice Test – Levels 9 and 10

CogAT® Practice Test - Sentence Completion

9. We often disagree because we think _____.

   A. strangely   B. differently   C. sometimes   D. apart   E. alike

10. Tim's baseball bat is _____ than mine, so I can't use it.

    A. wider   B. uglier   C. older   D. heavier   E. newer

11. No one wanted to go to the park due to the _____ playground.

    A. hidden   B. pristine   C. shabby   D. spotless   E. new

12. The _____ howled loudly outside my window, causing our flag to swing wildly.

    A. dog   B. wind   C. sleet   D. rain   E. snow

13. The school was at the edge of a large _____, with lots of shade for reading.

    A. meadow   B. pond   C. forest   D. swamp   E. river

14. Jane struggles with her homework, _____ when she has help from the teacher.

    A. only   B. even   C. just   D. sometimes   E. never

15. The boots were very thick and durable; they _____ Sam's feet.

    A. hurt   B. harmed   C. blistered   D. protected   E. broke

16. The food was _____ and those who ate it fell sick.

    A. delicious   B. cold   C. rotten   D. unappetizing   E. plentiful

CogAT® Practice Test - Sentence Completion

17. Once everyone arrives, we'll be able to _____ the museum's fascinating exhibits.

A. explore   B. purchase   C. boycott   D. skip   E. close

18. Not all animals are mammals, _____ all mammals are animals.

A. so   B. if   C. and   D. therefore   E. but

19. The girl in the park listened to the beautiful sound of birds _____ together.

A. screeching   B. laughing   C. chirping   D. flying   E. feeding

20. After many weeks, the _____ was over and the politician waited for the election results.

A. meeting   B. government   C. campaign   D. tour   E. war

Test 3:
Verbal Classifications

Test 3: Verbal Classification

Directions

For each question on this subtest, you need to identify how the three words in the question are related to one another. Once you have determined how the three words are alike, you need to choose the word among the answer choices that correctly belongs with the group of words in the question. There is only one answer choice that belongs with the correct verbal classification of the words in the question.

S1   milk   butter   yogurt   ?

A. cheese   B. salt   C. cereal   D. spoon   E. bacon

The first three words are **milk, butter,** and **yogurt**. How are these three words related to one another? Milk, butter, and yogurt are all dairy products. The only dairy product among the answer choices is **(A) cheese**. Salt, cereal, spoon, and bacon are not dairy products.

Find the **Test 3: Verbal Classification** section on your answer sheet. The first row of bubbles in this section is marked **S1**. Fill in the bubble labeled "A" in this row on your answer sheet.

Try to answer the second sample question on your own.

S2   book   magazine   pamphlet   ?

A. building   B. television   C. newspaper   D. pencil   E. eraser

The first three words are **book, magazine,** and **pamphlet**. How are these three words alike? Books, magazines, and pamphlets are all meant to be read. The only object among the answer choices that is meant to be read is a **(C) newspaper**. You should have filled in the bubble labeled "C" on the row marked **S2** on your answer sheet.

For each question on this subtest, you need to choose the word that belongs with the group of words. There is only one answer choice that belongs with the correct verbal classification of the words in the question.

Mark all of your answers in the **Test 3: Verbal Classification** section on your answer sheet. Make sure that you are on the correct question number on your answer sheet whenever you circle in your answer.

You will have ten minutes to complete this subtest. Try to answer every question. If you have trouble with a question, make an educated guess and move on to the next question. If you have time, you can go back to work on the questions you had trouble with. If you finish the Verbal Classification subtest early, you may check your work but do not go on to the next subtest.

CogAT® Practice Test - Verbal Classifications

1. banana   grapes   orange   ?

A. citrus   B. fruit   C. flower   D. apple   E. slice

2. quarter   dime   nickel   ?

A. money   B. silver   C. penny   D. wallet   E. cash

3. hammer   saw   screwdriver   ?

A. tool   B. dust   C. drill   D. nail   E. fix

4. water   tea   juice   ?

A. milk   B. drink   C. glass   D. thirst   E. sip

5. train   plane   truck   ?

A. transportation   B. boat   C. airport   D. travel   E. vacation

6. daffodil   geranium   daisy   ?

A. tulip   B. flower   C. garden   D. spring   E. bouquet

7. iceberg   igloo   snowman   ?

A. polar bear   B. melt   C. Arctic Circle   D. cold   E. icicles

8. worry   fret   doubt   ?

A. cry   B. concern   C. frown   D. feelings   E. angry

CogAT® Practice Test - Verbal Classifications

9. knife   fork   spatula   ?

A. pot   B. pan   C. plate   D. spoon   E. scissors

10. Saturn   Earth   Mars   ?

A. planet   B. comet   C. sun   D. Mercury   E. moon

11. summer   spring   autumn   ?

A. winter   B. cold   C. seasons   D. month   E. trip

12. diamond   ruby   onyx   ?

A. emerald   B. stone   C. ring   D. valuable   E. wear

13. pine   oak   maple   ?

A. bush   B. tree   C. elm   D. wood   E. forest

14. gymnastics   swimming   track   ?

A. football   B. skiing   C. basketball   D. hockey   E. soccer

15. pack   herd   pod   ?

A. animal   B. mammal   C. whale   D. wolf   E. colony

16. wheel   handles   pedal   ?

A. chain   B. saw   C. shoe   D. person   E. ride

CogAT® Practice Test - Verbal Classifications

17. babble   talk   speak   ?

A. pulsate   B. chatter   C. laugh   D. answer   E. think

18. Paris   London   San Francisco   ?

A. United States   B. country   C. city   D. globe   E. New York City

19. house   ranch   apartment   ?

A. garage   B. residence   C. cottage   D. meadow   E. garden

20. compass   barometer   odometer   ?

A. mug   B. measure   C. temperature   D. instrument   E. ruler

Test 4:
Number Analogies

Test 4: Number Analogies

Directions

For each question on this subtest, you need to figure out the relationship for each pair of numbers. Let's look at the first sample question.

S1   [1 → 3]   [6 → 8]   [11 → ?]

A. 8   B. 9   C. 10   D. 13   E. 14

In each bracket, there are two numbers with an arrow between them. The arrow informs you that something has been done to the first number to get the second number. In the first bracket, what do you do to the number "1" to get the number "3"? When you add 1 and 2 together, your sum is 3. In the second bracket, if you add 6 and 2 together, your sum is 8. The rule appears to be that you **add 2 to the first number in order to get the second number**. To find the number that belongs after the arrow in the third bracket, you need to add 2 to the first number in the bracket. 11 + 2 = 13. The correct answer choice is **(D) 13**.

Find the **Test 4: Number Analogies** section on your answer sheet. The first row of bubbles in this section is marked **S1**. Fill in the bubble labeled "D" in this row on your answer sheet. Try to answer the second sample question on your own.

S2   [16 → 12]   [10 → 6]   [22 → ?]

A. 24   B. 22   C. 20   D. 19   E. 18

In the first bracket, what do you do to the number "16" to get the number "12"? When you subtract 4 from 16, your difference is 12. In the second bracket, if you subtract 4 from 10, the difference is 6. The rule appears to be that you **subtract 4 from the first number in order to get the second number**. To find the number that belongs after the arrow in the third bracket, you need to subtract 4 from the first number in the bracket. 22 − 4 = 18. The correct answer choice is **(E) 18**. You should have filled in the bubble labeled "E" on the row marked **S2** on your answer sheet.

For each question on this subtest, you need to choose the number that belongs after the arrow in the third bracket. Mark all of your answers in the **Test 4: Number Analogies** section on your answer sheet. Make sure that you are on the correct question number on your answer sheet whenever you circle in your answer.

You will have ten minutes to complete this subtest. Try to answer every question. If you have trouble with a question, make an educated guess and move on to the next question. If you have time, you can go back to work on the questions you had trouble with. If you finish the Number Analogies subtest early, you may check your work but do not go on to the next subtest.

CogAT® Practice Test - Number Analogies

1. [2 → 4]   [4 → 6]   [10 → ?]

   A. 20   B. 18   C. 16   D. 12   E. 8

2. [2 → 5]   [6 → 9]   [11 → ?]

   A. 11   B. 14   C. 15   D. 16   E. 18

3. [5 → 4]   [6 → 5]   [7 → ?]

   A. 6   B. 7   C. 8   D. 9   E. 10

4. [4 → 8]   [5 → 9]   [6 → ?]

   A. 10   B. 11   C. 12   D. 13   E. 16

5. [1 → 8]   [3 → 10]   [5 → ?]

   A. 7   B. 10   C. 11   D. 12   E. 14

6. [12 → 9]   [18 → 15]   [22 → ?]

   A. 20   B. 19   C. 18   D. 17   E. 15

7. [20 → 14]   [18 → 12]   [14 → ?]

   A. 6   B. 7   C. 8   D. 10   E. 11

8. [6 → 3]   [8 → 4]   [10 → ?]

   A. 4   B. 5   C. 6   D. 8   E. 9

CogAT® Practice Test - Number Analogies

9. [20 → 10]   [15 → 5]   [10 → ?]

    A. 0   B. 5   C. 10   D. 15   E. 20

10. [15 → 21]   [18 → 24]   [21 → ?]

    A. 6   B. 20   C. 27   D. 28   E. 29

11. [1 → 4]   [2 → 7]   [4 → ?]

    A. 8   B. 11   C. 12   D. 13   E. 15

12. [4 → 18]   [6 → 20]   [8 → ?]

    A. 20   B. 21   C. 22   D. 23   E. 32

13. [21 → 7]   [32 → 18]   [40 → ?]

    A. 26   B. 20   C. 50   D. 8   E. 7

14. [18 → 10]   [16 → 9]   [14 → ?]

    A. 12   B. 10   C. 8   D. 7   E. 6

15. [7 → 4]   [9 → 5]   [13 → ?]

    A. 0   B. 1   C. 2   D. 7   E. 8

16. [30 → 12]   [40 → 17]   [50 → ?]

    A. 25   B. 23   C. 22   D. 20   E. 18

CogAT® Practice Test - Number Analogies

17. [34 → 9]   [55 → 30]   [46 → ?]

    A. 31   B. 30   C. 25   D. 22   E. 21

18. [53 → 18]   [61 → 26]   [72 → ?]

    A. 38   B. 37   C. 34   D. 32   E. 31

Test 5:
Number Puzzles

Test 5: Number Puzzles

Directions

For each question on this subtest, you need to choose the number that can be placed in the empty box to make both sides of the equation equal. Let's look at the first sample question.

S1

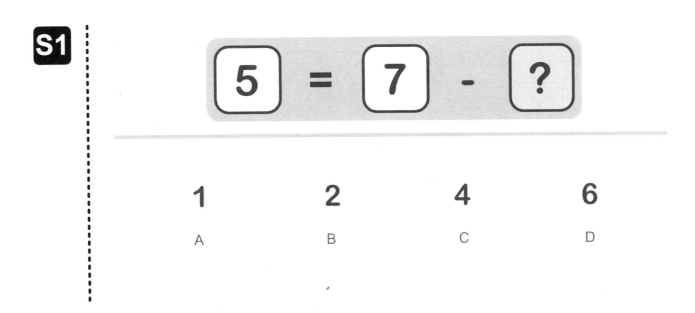

Both sides of the equation must total the same amount. The left side of the equation is 5. What number will subtract from 7 to get 5? You **subtract 2 from 7 to get 5** since 7 – 2 = 5. The correct answer choice is **(B) 2**.

Find the **Test 5: Number Puzzles** section on your answer sheet. The first row of bubbles in this section is marked **S1**. Fill in the bubble labeled "B" in this row on your answer sheet.

CogAT® Practice Test - Number Puzzles

Try to answer the second sample question on your own.

S2

$$8 = 4 + 1 + ?$$

2	3	4	5
A	B	C	D

The left side of the equation is 8. On the right side of the equation, 4 is added to 1 and another number. 4 + 1 = 5. What number can be added to 5 to get 8? You **add 3 to 5 to get 8** since 3 + 5 = 8. The correct answer choice is **(B) 3**. You should have filled in the bubble labeled "B" on the row marked **S2** on your answer sheet.

For each question on this subtest, you need to choose the number that can be placed in the empty box to make both sides of the equation equal. Mark all of your answers in the **Test 5: Number Puzzles** section on your answer sheet. Make sure that you are on the correct question number on your answer sheet whenever you circle in your answer.

You will have ten minutes to complete this subtest. Try to answer every question. If you have trouble with a question, make an educated guess and move on to the next question. If you have time, you can go back to work on the questions you had trouble with. If you finish the Number Puzzles subtest early, you may check your work but do not go on to the next subtest.

CogAT® Practice Test - Number Puzzles

01

[?] + [7] = [12]

8	7	6	5	4
A	B	C	D	E

02

[?] = [•] − [4]

[•] = [7]

1	2	3	4	5
A	B	C	D	E

03

[?] − [4] = [8]

8	9	10	11	12
A	B	C	D	E

CogAT® Practice Test - Number Puzzles

04

[?] − [•] = [5]

[•] = [1]

6	5	4	3	1
A	B	C	D	E

05

[?] = [•] + [9]

[•] = [5]

10	12	13	14	15
A	B	C	D	E

06

[?] − [•] = [4]

[•] = [3]

5	6	7	8	9
A	B	C	D	E

CogAT® Practice Test - Number Puzzles

07

? = • + 6

• = 1 + 2

7	8	9	10	12
A	B	C	D	E

08

? - • = 10

• = 12 - 2

10	18	20	22	24
A	B	C	D	E

09

? - • = 6

• = 3

9	8	7	6	5
A	B	C	D	E

CogAT® Practice Test - Number Puzzles

10

? × 2 = • + 3

• = 5 + 4

12	10	8	6	4
A	B	C	D	E

11

10 − ? = •

• = 5

3	4	5	6	7
A	B	C	D	E

12

? + 3 = •

• + 2 = 6

1	2	3	4	6
A	B	C	D	E

CogAT® Practice Test - Number Puzzles

13. ? = △ + 4
△ = 3 + △   • = 12

10	11	13	15	18
A	B	C	D	E

14. ? = △ + 6
20 = △ + •   4 = △ − •

6	8	13	14	18
A	B	C	D	E

15. ? = △ + 5
• = △ − 2   • = 5

11	12	13	16	18
A	B	C	D	E

CogAT® Practice Test - Number Puzzles

16 ? + 4 = 14 - △

△ = 5

1	2	4	5	6
A	B	C	D	E

Test 6:
Number Series

Quantitative Battery

Test 6: Number Series

Directions

For each question on this subtest, you are given a series of numbers which increase or decrease in a certain pattern. Once you have determined the pattern in the number series, you must choose the number that belongs after the arrow in the series.

S1   1   2   3   4   5   →

A. 6   B. 7   C. 8   D. 9   E. 10

Look at the series of numbers in the above sample. The series of numbers are **1, 2, 3, 4,** and **5**. What is happening to each number to get the next number in the series? **The rule is to add 1 to the previous number in order to get the next number in the series**. To find the number that belongs after the arrow in the number series, you need to add 1 to 5. 5 + 1 = 6. The correct answer choice is **(A) 6**.

Find the **Test 6: Number Series** section on your answer sheet. The first row of bubbles in this section is marked **S1**. Fill in the bubble labeled "A" in this row on your answer sheet.

Try to answer the second sample question on your own.

S2   12   9   6   3   →

A. 4   B. 3   C. 2   D. 1   E. 0

The series of numbers are **12, 9, 6,** and **3**. What is happening to each number to get the next number in the series? **The rule is to subtract 3 from the previous number in order to get the next number in the series**. To find the number that belongs after the arrow in the number series, you need to subtract 3 from 3. 3 – 3 = 0. The correct answer choice is **(E) 0**. You should have filled in the bubble labeled "E" on the row marked **S2** on your answer sheet.

For each question on this subtest, you need to choose the number that belongs after the arrow in the number series. Mark all of your answers in the **Test 6: Number Series** section on your answer sheet. Make sure that you are on the correct question number on your answer sheet whenever you circle in your answer.

You will have ten minutes to complete this subtest. Try to answer every question. If you have trouble with a question, make an educated guess and move on to the next question. If you have time, you can go back to work on the questions you had trouble with. If you finish the Number Series subtest early, you may check your work but do not go on to the next subtest.

On the actual Level 9 Number Series subtest, the first few questions will each have a picture of an abacus to the left of the number series. In this practice exam, these visual aids are not present since students for both levels of the exam will have to deal with number series without visual aids at some point in their respective subtests.

CogAT® Practice Test - Number Series

1. 2   4   8   16   32   →

   A. 74   B. 64   C. 54   D. 44   E. 14

2. 1   3   5   7   9   →

   A. 4   B. 8   C. 10   D. 11   E. 13

3. 5   4   3   5   4   3   →

   A. 1   B. 2   C. 3   D. 5   E. 6

4. 7   14   21   28   35   →

   A. 42   B. 49   C. 50   D. 51   E. 54

5. 21   17   13   9   5   →

   A. 5   B. 4   C. 3   D. 2   E. 1

6. $\frac{2}{8}$ $\frac{2}{10}$ $\frac{2}{12}$ $\frac{2}{14}$ $\frac{2}{16}$ →

   A. $\frac{2}{17}$ B. $\frac{2}{16}$ C. $\frac{2}{18}$ D. $\frac{2}{20}$ E. 2

7. 3   7   6   10   9   →

   A. 16   B. 15   C. 14   D. 13   E. 12

8. 2   4   5   7   8   →

   A. 9   B. 10   C. 11   D. 12   E. 13

CogAT® Practice Test - Number Series

9. 1   1   5   5   9   9   →

A. 15   B. 13   C. 12   D. 11   E. 10

10. 4   6   7   4   →

A. 6   B. 8   C. 9   D. 10   E. 11

11. 0   15   10   25   20   →

A. 40   B. 35   C. 30   D. 25   E. 20

12. 40   32   26   22   →

A. 18   B. 20   C. 24   D. 26   E. 30

13. 21   24   30   39   →

A. 42   B. 45   C. 48   D. 50   E. 51

14. 20   10   40   20   80   →

A. 20   B. 30   C. 32   D. 40   E. 60

15. 78   73   77   72   76   71   →

A. 70   B. 71   C. 72   D. 73   E. 75

16. 4   20   80   240   480   →

A. 120   B. 240   C. 420   D. 480   E. 500

17. **3   4   8   13   22** →

   A. 26   B. 28   C. 32   D. 36   E. 40

18. **24   24   22   23   20   22** →

   A. 14   B. 16   C. 18   D. 20   E. 23

Test 7:
Figure Matrices

Nonverbal Battery

Test 7: Figure Matrices

Directions

For each question on this subtest, you need to find the relationship between the figures in the top part of the square. Then, you must apply the same relationship to the figure or figures to the left of the arrow in the bottom part of the square to determine which figure belongs to the right of the arrow.

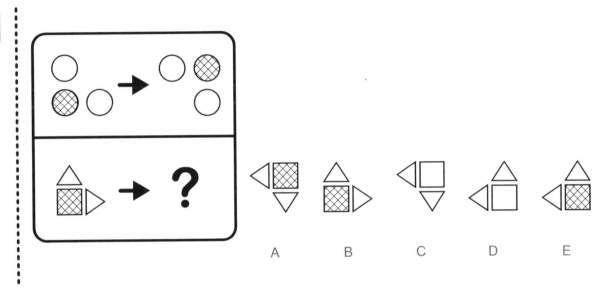

In the top part of the square, there are two figures. The figure to the left of the arrow consists of three circles in an "L" shape. The circle on the bottom left is criss-crossed. The figure to the right of the arrow is a **reflected image of the first figure that has been rotated 90 degrees counterclockwise**. In the bottom part of the square, there is a criss-crossed square with triangles above and to the right of the square. What will this figure look like if it is **reflected and then rotated 90 degrees counterclockwise?** If you were to **reflect** the image over to the right side of the arrow, you would have a criss-crossed square with triangles above and to the left of the square. Then, if you **rotated** the image 90 degrees counterclockwise, you would have a criss-crossed square with triangles to the left and below the square. This figure can be seen in **answer choice (A)**, so it is the correct answer.

Find the **Test 7: Figure Matrices** section on your answer sheet. The first row of bubbles in this section is marked **S1**. Fill in the bubble labeled "A" in this row on your answer sheet.

CogAT® Practice Test - Figure Matrices

Try to answer the second sample question on your own.

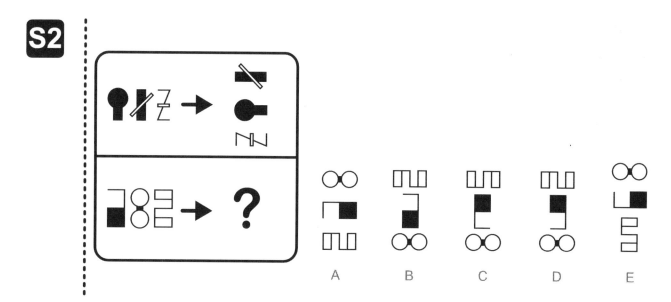

In the top part of the square, to the left of the arrow, there are a number of figures. How are these figures arranged to the right of the arrow? These figures are now **vertically aligned** and they have **switched positions**. The second figure is now the top figure, the first figure is the middle figure, and the third figure is the bottom figure. All of these figures have also been **rotated 90 degrees counterclockwise**. What would the figures in the bottom part of the square look like if they were to become **vertically aligned, switch positions,** and **rotate 90 degrees counterclockwise**. Well, to the right of the arrow, you would have the two circles on top, the middle figure would be the black and white rectangles, and the bottom figure would be the finished/unfinished rectangles. Since these figures need to be rotated 90 degrees counterclockwise, the circles will be to the left and right of each other in the top figure, the black rectangle will be to the right of the white rectangle, and the unfinished rectangles should be aligned horizontally. These figures can be seen in **answer choice (A)**, so it is the right answer. You should have filled in the bubble labeled "A" on the row marked **S2** on your answer sheet.

For each question on this subtest, you need to choose the figure or figures that belong after the arrow in the bottom part of the square. Mark all of your answers in the **Test 7: Figure Matrices** section on your answer sheet. Make sure that you are on the correct question number on your answer sheet whenever you circle in your answer.

You will have ten minutes to complete this subtest. Try to answer every question. If you have trouble with a question, make an educated guess and move on to the next question. If you have time, you can go back to work on the questions you had trouble with. If you finish the Figure Matrices subtest early, you may check your work but do not go on to the next subtest.

On the Level 9 Figure Matrices subtest, there are only 20 questions. Students who plan on taking the Level 9 exam may choose to stop after question #20 in this subtest. Students who plan on taking the Level 10 exam must attempt to answer all 22 questions in this subtest.

01

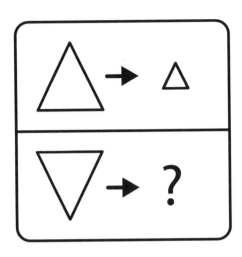

02

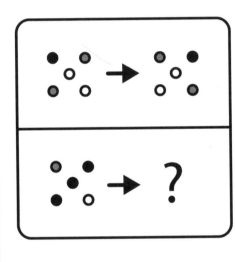
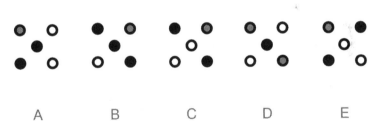

03

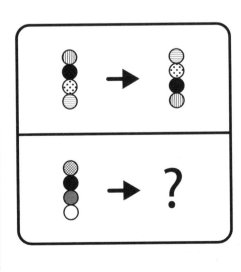

CogAT® Practice Test - Figure Matrices

04

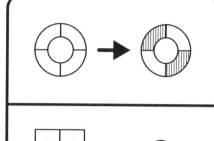

A   B   C   D   E

05

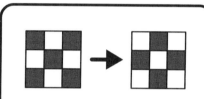

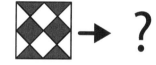

A   B   C   D   E

06

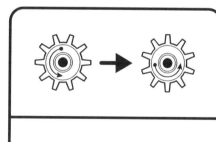

A   B   C   D   E

CogAT® Practice Test - Figure Matrices

07

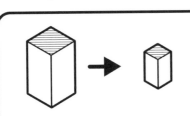

A B C D E

08

A B C D E

09

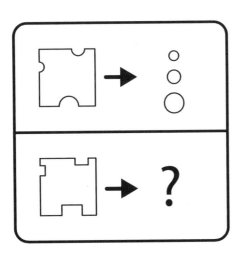

A B C D E

CogAT® Practice Test - Figure Matrices

10

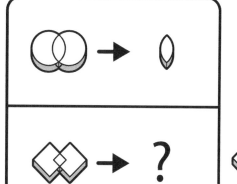

A B C D E

11

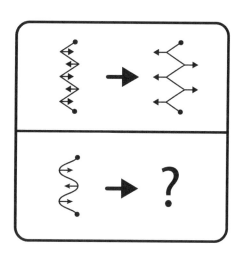

A B C D E

12

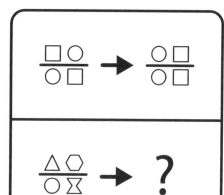

A B C D E

13

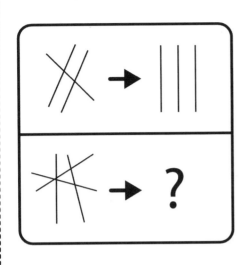

  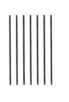 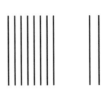

A   B   C   D   E

14

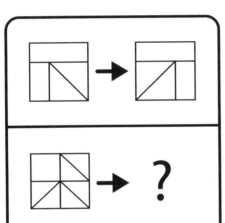

A   B   C   D   E

15

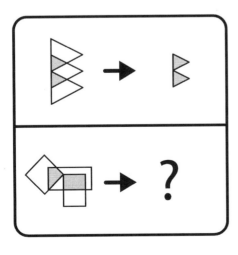

A   B   C   D   E

16

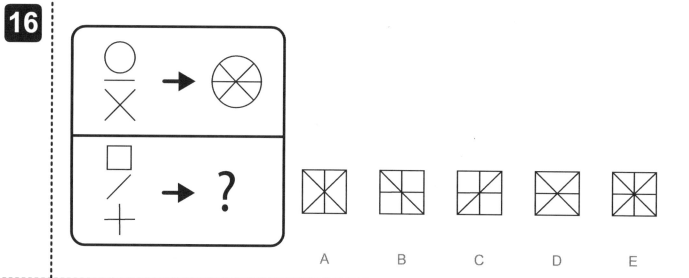

17

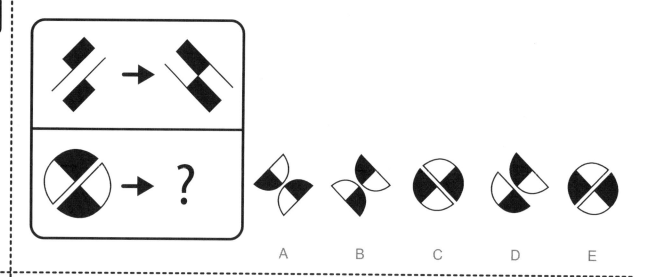

18

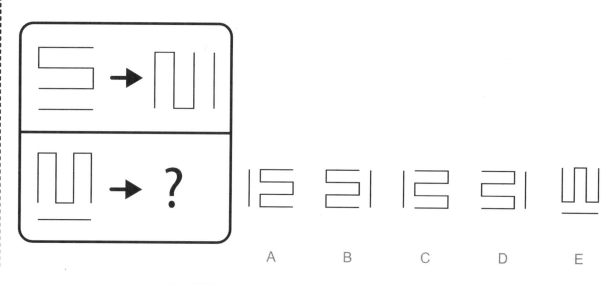

19

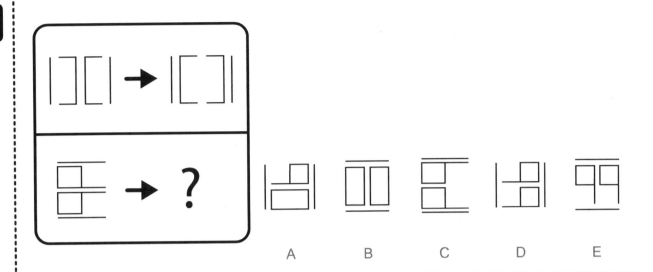

A   B   C   D   E

20

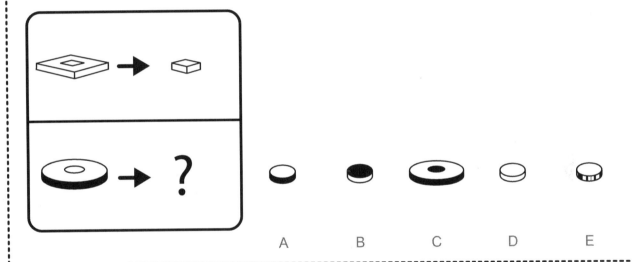

A   B   C   D   E

21

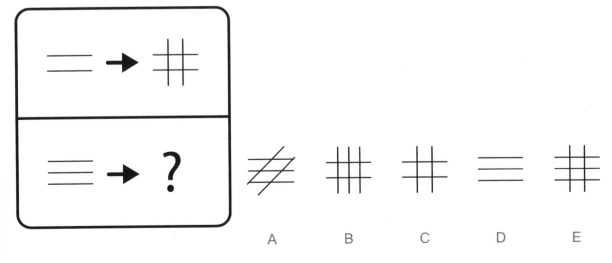

A   B   C   D   E

CogAT® Practice Test - Figure Matrices

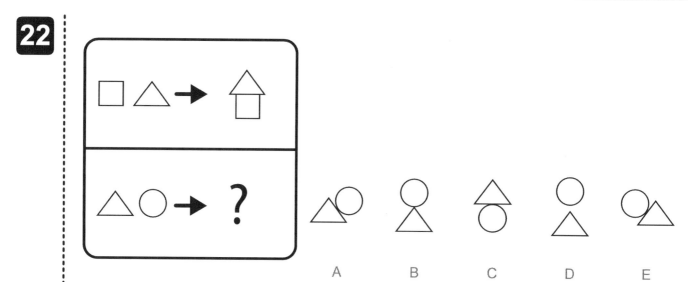

Test 8:
Paper Folding

Nonverbal Battery

Test 8: Paper Folding

Directions

For each question on this subtest, you are shown a piece of paper that is being folded. Then, a hole is punched into the folded piece of paper. You need to visualize what the paper will look like once it has been unfolded. Let's look at a sample question.

S1:

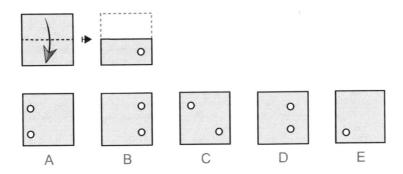

Look at the figure to the left of the arrow. It shows the way the paper looks before it is folded. The dotted lines show where the paper will be folded and the arrow shows the direction of the fold. In the above example, the paper will be folded so that the top half covers the bottom half. The figure to the right of the arrow shows the paper after it has been folded. The dotted lines show the paper size prior to the folding. The white circle shows where the hole has been punched in the paper.

Now, look at the answer choices. You must identify the figure that shows what the paper will look like after it is unfolded. Remember that the hole has been punched through two layers of paper. Thus, there must be two holes in the unfolded paper. Since the paper was folded in the vertical direction, the holes must be on top of one another. The hole was punched on the right side of the paper, so the holes in the unfolded paper must also be on the right side of the paper. The unfolded paper should look like the figure in **answer choice (B)**.

Find the **Test 8: Paper Folding** section on your answer sheet. The first row of bubbles in this section is marked **S1**. Fill in the bubble labeled "B" in this row on your answer sheet.

Try to answer the second sample question on your own.

S2:

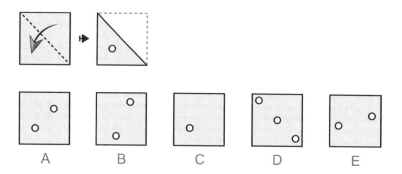

In the above example, what will the paper look like when it is unfolded? Well, the hole has been punched through two layers of paper, so there must be two holes in the unfolded paper. Since the paper was folded diagonally to the left, the holes should be diagonally aligned with one another in an upwards direction as you move from the left side to the right side of the paper. The unfolded paper should look like the figure in **answer choice (A)**. You should have filled in the bubble labeled "A" on the row marked **S2** on your answer sheet.

For each question on this subtest, you need to visualize what happens when a piece of paper is folded, a hole is cut in the paper, and the paper is unfolded. You must identify the answer choice that shows the figure of the unfolded paper. Mark all of your answers in the **Test 8: Paper Folding** section on your answer sheet. Make sure that you are on the correct question number on your answer sheet whenever you circle in your answer.

You will have ten minutes to complete this subtest. Try to answer every question. If you have trouble with a question, make an educated guess and move on to the next question. If you have time, you can go back to work on the questions you had trouble with. If you finish the Paper Folding subtest early, you may check your work but do not go on to the next subtest.

CogAT® Practice Test - Paper Folding

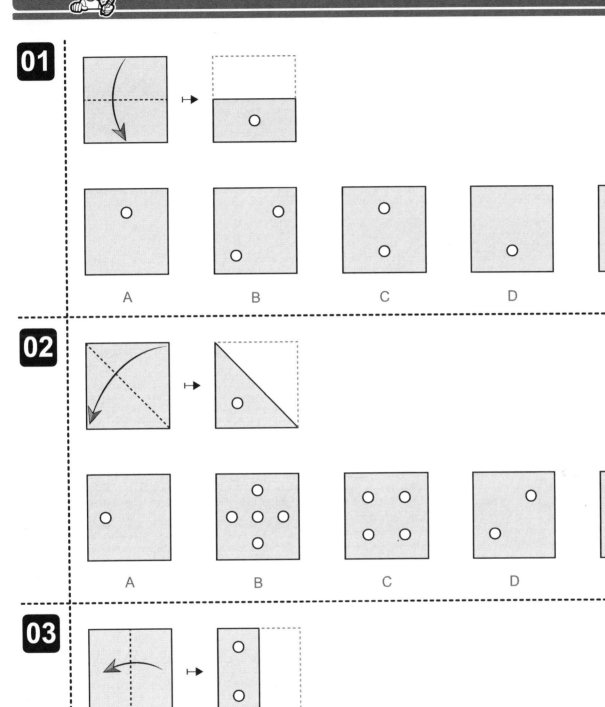

CogAT® Practice Test - Paper Folding

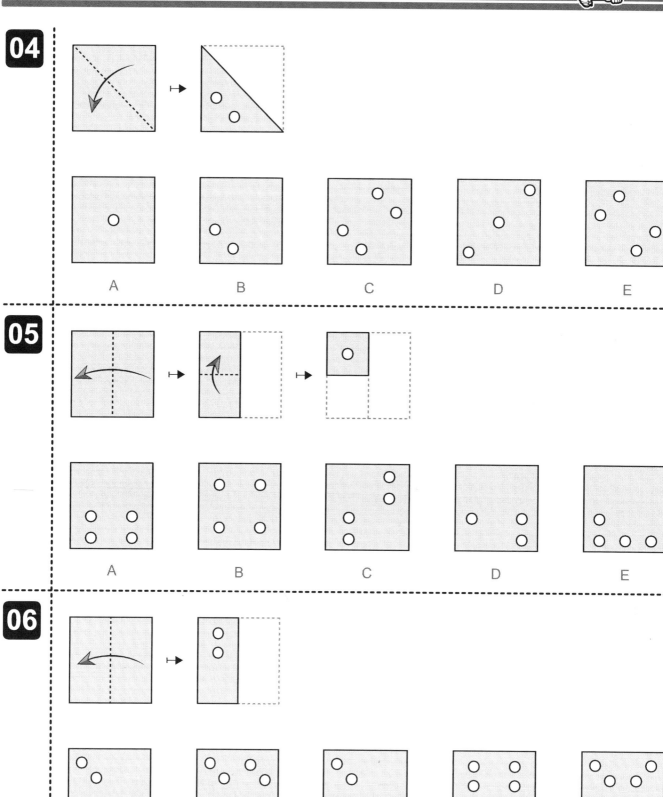

CogAT® Practice Test - Paper Folding

07
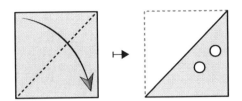

 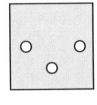 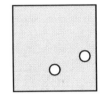 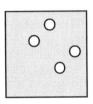 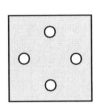
A   B   C   D   E

08
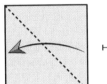 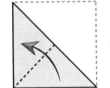

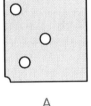 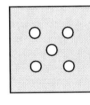 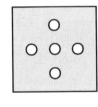 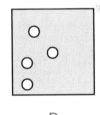 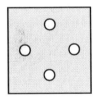
A   B   C   D   E

09
  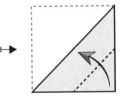

  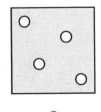 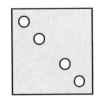 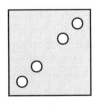
A   B   C   D   E

Bright Kids NYC Inc. ©   **CogAT® Practice Test – Levels 9 and 10**

CogAT® Practice Test - Paper Folding

10

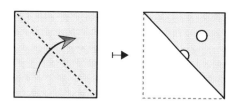

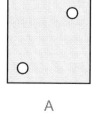 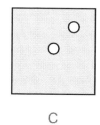 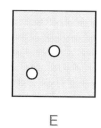
A B C D E

11

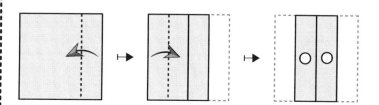

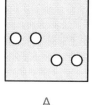 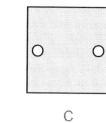 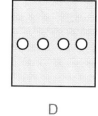 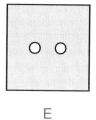
A B C D E

12

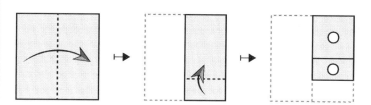

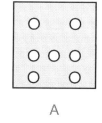 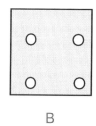 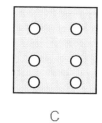 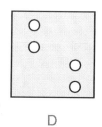 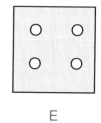
A B C D E

CogAT® Practice Test – Levels 9 and 10

13

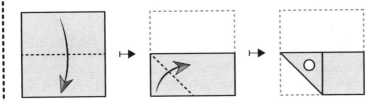

 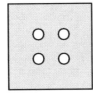  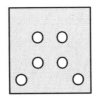 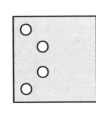

A B C D E

14

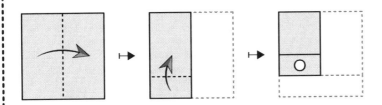

 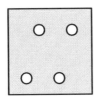 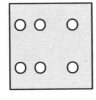

A B C D E

15

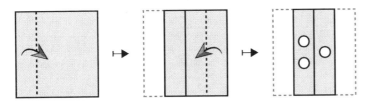

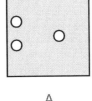 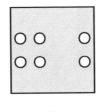

A B C D E

16

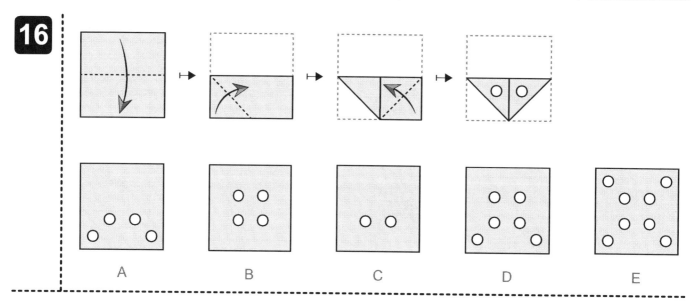

Test 9:
Figure Classifications

Nonverbal Battery

Test 9: Figure Classification

Directions

For each question on this subtest, you are presented with three figures. You must select the figure among the answer choices that belongs with the set of figures. Let's look at a sample question.

S1:

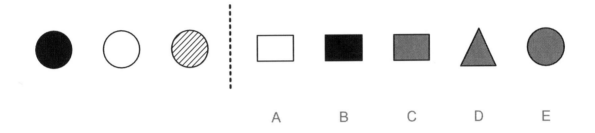

There are three figures to the left of the vertical line. How are these three figures alike? Well, all three of these figures are circles that have different types of shading. The figure that belongs with this set must be a circle that is not white, black, or striped. Thus, the gray circle belongs with this set of figures. **Answer choice (E)** is correct.

Find the **Test 9: Figure Classification** section on your answer sheet. The first row of bubbles in this section is marked **S1**. Fill in the bubble labeled "E" in this row on your answer sheet.

CogAT® Practice Test - Figure Classifications

Try to answer the second sample question on your own.

S2:

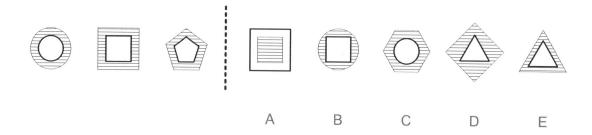

A   B   C   D   E

How are the three figures to the left of the vertical line alike? Each figure has the same shape within a shape. The smaller shape is white and the larger shape is striped. So, you are looking for a figure that has the same white shape within a larger striped shape. The figure in answer choice (E) is a small white triangle inside a larger striped triangle. Thus, **answer choice (E)** is correct. You should have filled in the bubble labeled "E" on the row marked **S2** on your answer sheet.

For each question on this subtest, you need to select the figure among the answer choices that belongs with the set of figures to the left of the vertical line. Mark all of your answers in the **Test 9: Figure Classification** section on your answer sheet. Make sure that you are on the correct question number on your answer sheet whenever you circle in your answer.

You will have ten minutes to complete this subtest. Try to answer every question. If you have trouble with a question, make an educated guess and move on to the next question. If you have time, you can go back to work on the questions you had trouble with. If you finish the Figure Classification subtest early, you may check your work but do not go on to the next subtest.

On the Level 9 Figure Classification subtest, there are only 20 questions. Students who plan on taking the Level 9 exam may choose to stop after question #20 in this subtest. Students who plan on taking the Level 10 exam must attempt to answer all 22 questions in this subtest.

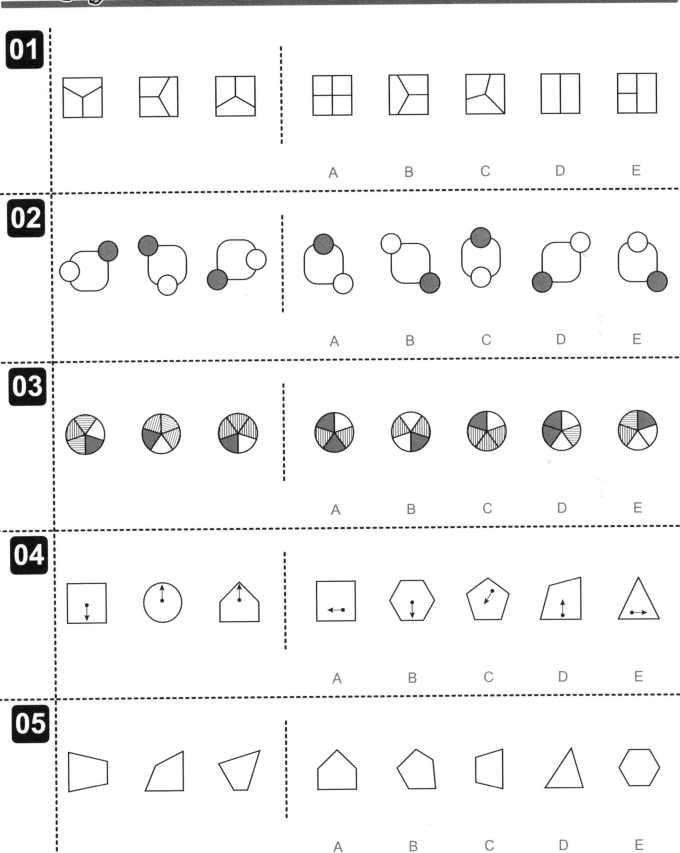

CogAT® Practice Test - Figure Classifications

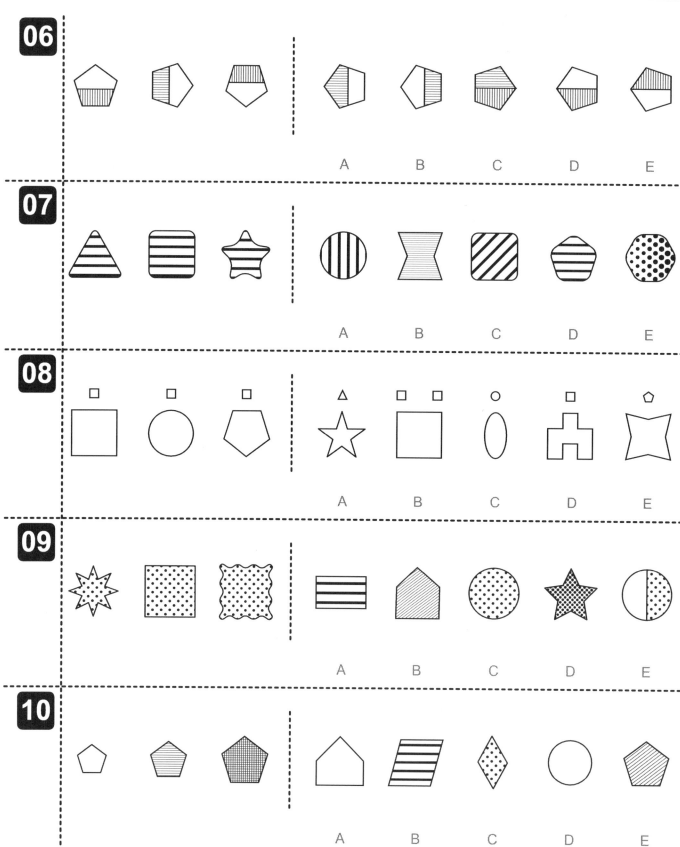

11

   |

　　　　　　　　　　　　　　A　　　B　　　C　　　D　　　E

12

   |

　　　　　　　　　　　　　　A　　　B　　　C　　　D　　　E

13

   |

　　　　　　　　　　　　　　A　　　B　　　C　　　D　　　E

14

   |

　　　　　　　　　　　　　　A　　　B　　　C　　　D　　　E

15

   |

　　　　　　　　　　　　　　A　　　B　　　C　　　D　　　E

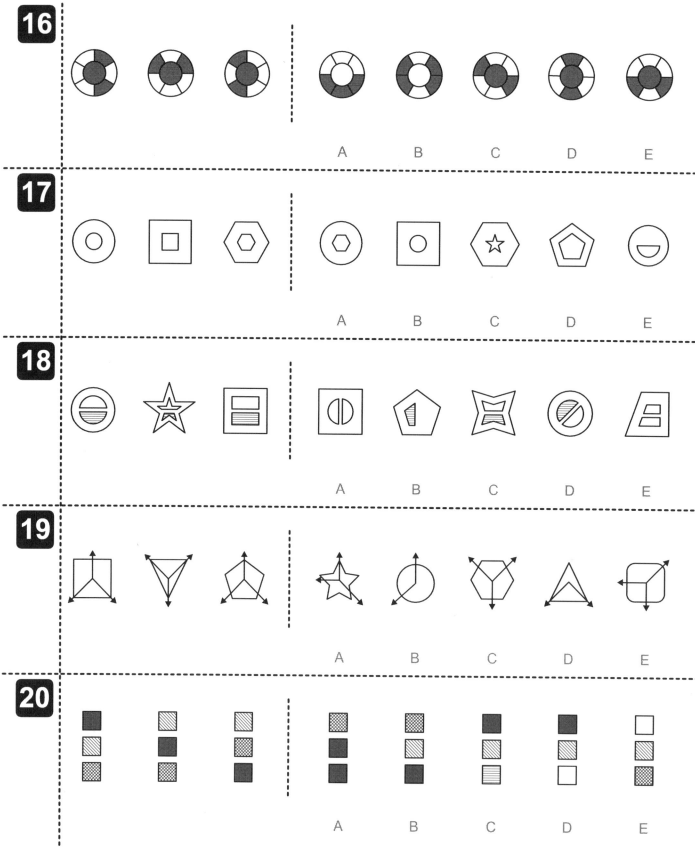

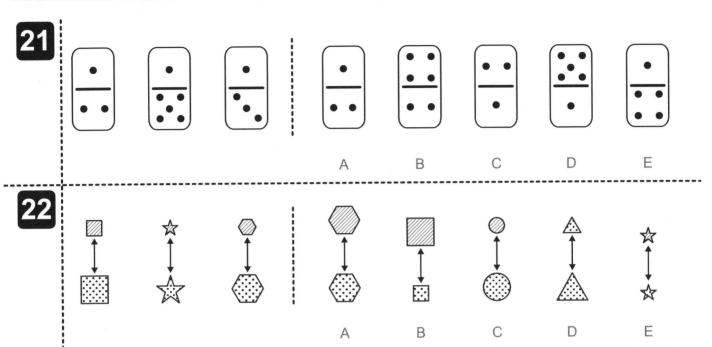

Answer Key

Answer Key

	VA	SC	VC	NA	NP	NS	FM	PF	FC
1.	B	E	D	D	D	B	A	C	B
2.	B	B	C	B	C	D	B	D	E
3.	D	C	C	A	E	D	C	D	C
4.	A	E	A	A	A	A	E	C	B
5.	A	B	B	D	D	E	B	B	C
6.	C	B	A	B	C	C	A	D	B
7.	D	A	E	C	C	D	D	D	D
8.	D	A	B	B	C	B	B	E	D
9.	E	B	D	A	A	B	A	D	C
10.	B	D	D	C	D	A	C	B	E
11.	B	C	A	B	C	B	E	D	C
12.	E	B	A	C	A	B	A	C	D
13.	A	C	C	A	C	E	B	E	E
14.	B	B	B	C	E	D	C	A	D
15.	C	D	E	E	B	E	A	E	E
16.	B	C	A	C	D	D	C	E	E
17.	C	A	B	E		D	B		D
18.	E	E	E	B		C	B		C
19.	A	C	C				C		C
20.	A	C	E				A		B
21.	A						E		E
22.	D						B		C
23.	A								
24.	E								

Answer Sheets

Quantitative Battery

Sample Questions
- S1. Ⓐ Ⓑ Ⓒ Ⓓ Ⓔ
- S2. Ⓐ Ⓑ Ⓒ Ⓓ Ⓔ

Test 4: Number Analogies
1. Ⓐ Ⓑ Ⓒ Ⓓ Ⓔ
2. Ⓐ Ⓑ Ⓒ Ⓓ Ⓔ
3. Ⓐ Ⓑ Ⓒ Ⓓ Ⓔ
4. Ⓐ Ⓑ Ⓒ Ⓓ Ⓔ
5. Ⓐ Ⓑ Ⓒ Ⓓ Ⓔ
6. Ⓐ Ⓑ Ⓒ Ⓓ Ⓔ
7. Ⓐ Ⓑ Ⓒ Ⓓ Ⓔ
8. Ⓐ Ⓑ Ⓒ Ⓓ Ⓔ
9. Ⓐ Ⓑ Ⓒ Ⓓ Ⓔ
10. Ⓐ Ⓑ Ⓒ Ⓓ Ⓔ
11. Ⓐ Ⓑ Ⓒ Ⓓ Ⓔ
12. Ⓐ Ⓑ Ⓒ Ⓓ Ⓔ
13. Ⓐ Ⓑ Ⓒ Ⓓ Ⓔ
14. Ⓐ Ⓑ Ⓒ Ⓓ Ⓔ
15. Ⓐ Ⓑ Ⓒ Ⓓ Ⓔ
16. Ⓐ Ⓑ Ⓒ Ⓓ Ⓔ
17. Ⓐ Ⓑ Ⓒ Ⓓ Ⓔ
18. Ⓐ Ⓑ Ⓒ Ⓓ Ⓔ

Sample Questions
- S1. Ⓐ Ⓑ Ⓒ Ⓓ Ⓔ
- S2. Ⓐ Ⓑ Ⓒ Ⓓ Ⓔ

Test 5: Number Puzzles
1. Ⓐ Ⓑ Ⓒ Ⓓ Ⓔ
2. Ⓐ Ⓑ Ⓒ Ⓓ Ⓔ
3. Ⓐ Ⓑ Ⓒ Ⓓ Ⓔ
4. Ⓐ Ⓑ Ⓒ Ⓓ Ⓔ
5. Ⓐ Ⓑ Ⓒ Ⓓ Ⓔ
6. Ⓐ Ⓑ Ⓒ Ⓓ Ⓔ
7. Ⓐ Ⓑ Ⓒ Ⓓ Ⓔ
8. Ⓐ Ⓑ Ⓒ Ⓓ Ⓔ
9. Ⓐ Ⓑ Ⓒ Ⓓ Ⓔ
10. Ⓐ Ⓑ Ⓒ Ⓓ Ⓔ
11. Ⓐ Ⓑ Ⓒ Ⓓ Ⓔ
12. Ⓐ Ⓑ Ⓒ Ⓓ Ⓔ
13. Ⓐ Ⓑ Ⓒ Ⓓ Ⓔ
14. Ⓐ Ⓑ Ⓒ Ⓓ Ⓔ
15. Ⓐ Ⓑ Ⓒ Ⓓ Ⓔ
16. Ⓐ Ⓑ Ⓒ Ⓓ Ⓔ

Sample Questions
- S1. Ⓐ Ⓑ Ⓒ Ⓓ Ⓔ
- S2. Ⓐ Ⓑ Ⓒ Ⓓ Ⓔ

Test 6: Number Series
1. Ⓐ Ⓑ Ⓒ Ⓓ Ⓔ
2. Ⓐ Ⓑ Ⓒ Ⓓ Ⓔ
3. Ⓐ Ⓑ Ⓒ Ⓓ Ⓔ
4. Ⓐ Ⓑ Ⓒ Ⓓ Ⓔ
5. Ⓐ Ⓑ Ⓒ Ⓓ Ⓔ
6. Ⓐ Ⓑ Ⓒ Ⓓ Ⓔ
7. Ⓐ Ⓑ Ⓒ Ⓓ Ⓔ
8. Ⓐ Ⓑ Ⓒ Ⓓ Ⓔ
9. Ⓐ Ⓑ Ⓒ Ⓓ Ⓔ
10. Ⓐ Ⓑ Ⓒ Ⓓ Ⓔ
11. Ⓐ Ⓑ Ⓒ Ⓓ Ⓔ
12. Ⓐ Ⓑ Ⓒ Ⓓ Ⓔ
13. Ⓐ Ⓑ Ⓒ Ⓓ Ⓔ
14. Ⓐ Ⓑ Ⓒ Ⓓ Ⓔ
15. Ⓐ Ⓑ Ⓒ Ⓓ Ⓔ
16. Ⓐ Ⓑ Ⓒ Ⓓ Ⓔ
17. Ⓐ Ⓑ Ⓒ Ⓓ Ⓔ
18. Ⓐ Ⓑ Ⓒ Ⓓ Ⓔ

Nonverbal Battery

Test 7: Figure Matrices — Sample Questions S1, S2; Questions 1–22

Test 8: Paper Folding — Sample Questions S1, S2; Questions 1–16

Test 9: Figure Classification — Sample Questions S1, S2; Questions 1–22z